WHERE IS MY MONEY GOING?

One Week Mindset Challenge

By

Sharon Adundo

FINANCIAL HIKERS

The power in saving.

Dedication

This is a simplified interactive version of self-evaluation for easier understanding to help jumpstart a change in your financial life. Simple plain terms have also been used with no complicated financial terms to help with the basics that one needs to consider. I had a problem earlier in my life of big books. I thought of the challenges I had in school reading big books that were sometimes discouraging as I sought the deeper meaning of what was being communicated. I know am not alone in this. Therefore, this is a special consideration to accommodate anyone who might be or was in the same position as I was to make it easier to read and solve a problem at hand.

Contents

Preface

I have always had an inner pressure to motivate and inspire others and share what I know as I learn from others too.

I love empowering, and looking for like-minded people too. I love little things that can motivate one to stop thinking as if that's the end of the world. I have gone through a lot myself but never did I let the low moments pin me down. I have little survival tactics that enabled me to be who I am. I studied business with a concentration in Finance and realized that most people have no point of inspiration and motivation to excel in what they do. Finance is a major part that people are scared to talk about based on differently formed opinions which hurt progress. I therefore saw the need to empower more people to think independently.

So far...I have started with SAVINGS as the first reference point because it is a line we ignore to handle because we have so much on our plate to deal with. ...

Sometimes, it's easier said than done so it can be helpful if we check on each other just to get a little motivation at least to work on the target and make sure the savings transfer is done regardless...as we share other financial areas that are crucial in our lives.

Remember FINANCE can be a very boring topic to discuss when one starts plotting graphs and figures which might end up not being received well. So let's talk freely about it including ways to boost our lines of specialization.

Sad reality is that, in the current economy, majority of what we NEED in life is all money related. We have to have money in most cases in order to get what we NEED. Money topic is a MUST TALK in our lives at the moment.

WHEN someone keeps hammering in your ears every day, every time, sending reminders to you to plan and budget and yet you are financially challenged at that particular time, you can easily turn off the notifications from that person. WHAT will happen in the end? Blocking the possibilities of ATTACKING the problem existing and finding the solution to the issue in question.

This is boring indeed, but do not give up.

Remember that we need to focus and find a way of working on at least seven streams of income in our lives....one might not be enough to take care of our needs.

Statistics shows that many people LACK savings account. We do not have to wait till we get a lot of money in order to start saving. No money is too little to manage.

Apparently, $1+1=2...$
It is the same ever since I started learning so is financial life. The difference is that mathematics instructions require us to think a little extra as in the case of $x+1/2y=6$, find X.

So where is your X?

My Financial Journey

It all started as a dream and a wish when I was in 5th grade. It led to having a pen pal, hard work, admiring kids acting in the TV programs. My wish to come to America and drive a car was real. I just wanted to drive a car and go back to my motherland Kenya. I thought owning a car in Kenya at a lower age wasn't possible as kids in the movie in the states.

I had a focused mindset that was heavily focusing on ways to come to America. I worked hard, at a tender age, I sold stuff that includes; water, candies, ice / frozen water, rubbed used stamps and reselling, made handmade wall hangings, calligraphic writings and many more....All this done in the name of saving for the American dream. After college graduation no better job opportunity was forthcoming. I finally landed a job that provided basic needs. This is where I learned to survive within my means. I rented a bedsitter (studio) where I could see all my belongings at a glance and life went on. In my tiny room, I learned to maximize my space mostly at night and over the weekend as my side hustle. I bought plain fabric in wholesale, made batik / art decorations and sold them. Through sales, I started saving for my American dream. Reading on the side too to learn more about what I needed to do to get to where I wanted to be.

I finally got my best option for school selection to further my studies and landed in TROY Alabama. This was another major transition in my life. Life was unbearable for I knew nobody in that area apart from friends that I made. I did odd jobs to survive and volunteering to activities to get going.

Through the struggles, I became a mother of two, before finishing my education that I was pursuing. I had to learn to plan and survive no Matter what for I couldn't let my dream die. I struggled with my budget to make things work out. Child care has no flexibility in this country. I had to quit my job to RESET and plan for my kids' future which took a lot of sacrifice and hardship. At some point, I lived on free food offered by the community I lived in which I had to keep as a secret because of the stigma that people associate those who get free food with go through. I also survived on thrift shopping. Through this, I came up with different ways of disciplined budgeting that enabled me to make it through with my kids and family.

I learned to survive on nothing to bare minimum. I learned to cut my coat according to my sleeve. I had to survive with commission jobs that had no guarantee of any income but my efforts. This is where I learned to formulate a plan and get out of the deep hole that was burying me alive.

Shaking off the dust and moving on, I took control of my financial life and I started this journey. I would like to share with you my journey with the hope of transforming and inspiring you to take control of your situation now.

Day 1

Self-Analysis

Day 1
Self –Analysis

According to Merriam-Webster, Self –analysis is a systematic attempt by an individual to understand his or her own persona ity without the aid of another person. You are in Financial Journey self-discovery. This is your own honest opinion as to who you are according to your own understanding financially.

This is the introductory part of the whole journey you are about to embark on. Look into your financial life and analyze where you currently belong.

I was caught up in a situation whereby I had to start all over one more time. I was in a big dilemma of letting go. The fear of unknowns and what if's kept racing in my mind. This was the toughest decision I wasn't willing to accommodate. I had to decide whether I let go my Precious business that I established when things went sour or not. I dic not have a plan B at that particular time. I was helpless and stressed out. I had kids who depended on me, I was studying for my masters, I didn't want to drop out and fail in all areas. I had to get my senses back together and take responsibility of who I am and what my worth is. I had to sit down one more time and think like a functioning humanity.

Have you ever been in a situation whereby you are hopeless and you do not know what to do and cannot think anymore? Have you ever felt like being squeezed in a corner and no air to breathe to keep living and the only thing coming in your mind and keeps repeating itself is that you cannot make it? Yes this can be so dangerous and a proper U-turn planning is the rescue that got me out of this ditch.

I had to sit down one more time and think, I had to literally write down all the thoughts that I was thinking of and separate the negative from the positive. This was my next journey to realization of where I belonged financially.

In order to accomplish this process, take time to respond to the questions below.

Questions to ask yourself and be honest with your answers despite your status;

a) Do you have any emergency funds?

....

b) Do you have any savings?

....

c) Are you monitoring your daily spending?

....
.

d) Have you managed to come up with new ways to evaluate what's important and what's not in your financial life?

....
.

- If you have, what are the ways you use?

....
....

- If you have not, would you consider learning?

....
e) How many streams of income do you have?

....

....

f) Are you happy with your current Financial Status?

....

.

Important notes you would like to consider day 1.

1...
...

2...
...

3...
...

4...
...

5...
...

Sleep over it

Financial journey is a process. Consistency and determination lead to a breakthrough. You have to keep repeating the same discipline over and over.

Day 2

Budgeting and Planning

Day 2
Budgeting and Planning

What is a budget and a plan?

A budget is a formulated plan on how the available money can be spent or will be spent.

On the other hand, a plan is a thought processed idea laid down to be implemented.

After first day review of your financial position and answering the questions portion, you are in a better position to forge ahead on WHAT'S NEXT FOR YOU? This is the phase you will need to start writing down ALL that revolves around you financially related.

Areas to cover include;

Are you a student, employed, self-employed or not employed?

....

Do you have any source of income? This will include any money coming in that include; salary, commission, donation or pocket money, est.

....

What is your income range?

....
....

Categorizing your income

-We have Fixed-income (for those that have specific monthly income whether working or not working).

....
....
....
....

-Variable income (for those paid by commission or self-employed...including side hustle income).

....
....
....
....

What bills do you have?

Categorize your expenses.

-We have fixed expenses (they are specific each month. They include; tithe, rent, phone bills, insurance, loan payment, daycare, cable/internet, e.t.c)

....
....
....
....
....

-Variable expenses (figures changes based on usage or are unpredictable. They include; tithe, gas / fuel, water bill, electricity, food, parking fee, tolls, miscellaneous).

....
....
....
....
....

.

Do you have any Investments?

An Investment is an asset or an item that is bought with the hope of generating income or appreciating in the future. This includes; Land, Shares, Any property, Insurance cover, e.t.c. You can list them down.

....
....
....
....
....
....

How much debt do you have (list them)?

....
....
....
....
....
....

How is your credit score like?

....
....

Based on the above-listed responses, looking at the expenses portion and debt versus income available, where are you currently situated? You will have to add up all your income and then add all your listed expenses/ debt then subtract your expenses/ debt from your income. Are you living over the limit or under the limit? When living under the limit, you will have some change after subtraction, while when you are living over the limit, you will have a negative sign after subtraction.

....
....
....

Is everything listed on your expense portion necessary?

....

....

...

List areas you can eliminate or cut cost on to help reduce debts if you have debts to pay?

....

....

....

....

....

We all have to incur expenditure at some point in life irrespective of our status. At one point we do money exchange and we are responsible for the transaction that takes place between the two or more parties involved. It is at this point that we all need to take responsibility and always be sensible in what we do with what we have at hand or what we are assigned to use. Take a look again at what you have listed above and make sure that it reflects your current situation to help you move to the next level of self-realization.

Day 3

Daily Spending Check

Day 3
Daily Spending Check

In order to tackle the root cause of financial hiccup, you have to start with the very moment you wake up from the bed and start using stuff around you till the time you go back to sleep. This will help track on little spending habits in a day that piles up to be a daily routine.

Take a look at your life today. What do you do? What do you use? How many of the expenditure related deals were planned for? Consider all the activities you engaged in that are money related. Some are at times taken for granted but they end up adding up big time.

On your third day of the journey, do a Random DAY WATCH ON Spending and answer the questions below at the end of the day.

Did you spend money today?

....

If you did, how much did you spent?
-List down all you bought or paid for. Don't forget the little candy, water, snacks, gum, crackers, chips, e.t.c.

....
....
....
....
....
....
-Were they all necessary?

....
....
...

Where did you buy from?

....
....

-What could have been the price if you bought it somewhere else other than where you bought it from? (Do a little research - quick stop shopping places are normally expensive as compared to major stores).

....
....
....
....

Could you have saved any coin if you had planned for the same on your weekly or daily planner?

....
....

(Use this approach and evaluate yourself from today on a daily basis and analyze if you can realize a little change).

Day 4

Get to Work

Day 4
Get to Work

Take control of your financial life NOW….. Go back to your list on Day two and three.

Where do you stand as at now? Are you in debt or out of debt?

....

....

......

After evaluation, how is your mindset up to this point? Are you in a position to work out a plan or in a confused status due to too many issues to handle?

....

....

......

Is there anything you can do to cut down expenses listed so far?

....

....

....

......

Did you list that you have debt? If so, how are you tackling the debts?

....

....

....

....

....

This is the point whereby you need to look at what can be eliminated, substituted, reduced, in order to use the cash difference to settle a debt and build up a savings Emergency account.

Savings Tips

-Stop buying anything without planning or budgeting for it.

- Always buy when it's really necessary.

-Don't go shopping when too hungry, it leads to too much unnecessary spending of unbudgeted items.

-Avoid paying bills beyond the due dates if you can. Payments after due dates normally incur extra fee or high-interest rates that adds up and eat your savings.

-Negotiate on payments if you can't make it by due date. Find out if they can excuse you from late fee charges.

-Negotiate for a lower interest charge if they have to charge you past your due date payment period.

-Review your bills eliminate those that you can do without. If you have a service provider, ask for better deal or specials provided with the intention to get a good deal at a lower price. If a bill is discontinued or lowered in rate, divert that the money into your savings account.

Did you also know that you can negotiate on some bank charges and get full refund on fees they charge? Yes, they do refund just learn the best approach on the fee in question.

Mind Jogging!!!!

One might say; "My income is still the same, I can't save because I still have debts to pay. I will start saving after clearing my debts".

This is a NO –it's a killer in savings mindset. THE TRUTH IS, SAVINGS IS NEEDED REGARDLESS OF THE DEBT WE HAVE. MAKE SAVINGS PORTION TO BE LIKE ANOTHER MONTHLY PAYMENT.

Another person might say; "I have no extra money, my budget is still tight, I will save when I get a pay increase or a better job".

STOP AND REFLECT! WHAT MAKES YOUR BUDGET SO TIGHT? PLEASE LIST YOUR BUDGET DOWN AND CHECK ON AREA THAT CAN BE LOOSENED. **There will never be a time in life when you will have enough money. Money cycle expands. The more money you get, the more it stretches to cover other commitments. So start the discipline now.**

Examples of what you need to look at to help tap little savings.

1. Insurance; negotiate and look for new deals or specials that include lower rates for better coverage.

2. Electricity; Turn on the lights when it's necessary. Switch off the lights when an area is not in use. Also, learn to regulate the thermostat for those using it as air conditioning or heating options.

3. Limit eating junk food you find that most of them in convenience stores got high rates.

4. Learn to cook and eat from home. The example that will help you understand the concept is, pack your breakfast and lunch. Stop buying ready-made food. Try this for one week and calculate what you can save at the end of the week. Make sure you write down what your daily spending is for the food purchased and cooked at home. Also write how much you could have spent while eating out. Get the difference in the amount saved.

5. Learn to control swiping your ATM or credit cards. If you can't control swiping your credit card, freeze it in the freezer (put in a ziplock with water).

Is this your current situation!

Debt can hinder progress in life if there is no proper plan in place, to monitor it making sure that it's paid down. Emphasis is given on DEBT to help tackle it without assuming that it will pay itself or someone else will pay it for you. Debt impact therefore, makes one to continue sinking and getting stressed thinking of how to pay IT instead of thinking of new ways to get better. You have to tackle this part if in debt, If you are not in debt; consider formulating a working plan to make sure that all spending is accounted for and tracked.

Sometimes after exploring the above-listed ways of re-strategizing, you might still feel the pressure of things that needs to be taken care of. When you have a negative balance after calculating income and expenditure, you can explore other ways to help generate extra income. This will help absorb the negative balance.

What are the little boosts you can consider to help generate quick cash when you have a negative balance or an emergency situation?

Here you will need a quick fix sometimes to help cover the situation without digging more into debts. There are some moments in life that needs quick thinking and innovation. You need to write down other income options you could consider besides what you are currently doing.

"Example; My side hustle/mixed business includes; online dispatch/load search commission based, online sales, ladies selections (bags, watches, jewelry, tops, pants e.t.c according to the season), drop deliveries once in a while, selling at friendly functions (carrying few products), e.tc. Remember one thing....side hustle are little income substitutes which have minimal profit on an item. Do not expect to get high return on just an item...it's an accumulation of little pennies in a collective pool to help substitute a need."

Now take your time and list that which you would consider exploring in order to act as a substitute for your income. If you already have one in place then, consider ways you can help boost it and be consistent with it. You can easily achieve this by studying the people around you. What they would benefit from or need most at that particular area. An example is, if you are close to a construction site, check if they will need some quick food or drinks, analyze their budget range, calculate to see is you can provide some rice, beans, water and still make profit out of it.

If you are working in a warehouse, you can make some jelly sandwich and sell some during lunch hours. If you are next to a busy university, consider offering part-time editing and mobile stationary supplies. If you are next to a school, consider looking into grocery and stationery supplies and many others.

Do you have anything to consider at this point as your income substitute?

....

....

....

....

Is It Too Overwhelming?

Day 5
Is It Too Overwhelming?

Financial journey can be stressful after realizing that it's time to make a change and make a difference. It can lead to heart race feeling and some pressure within if options seem to be tight to work with. This is the point of realization that CHANGE is necessary.

On this special day, gather what you need to work with through this journey. You will need to have a yearly planner to help with daily planning and a separate notebook to draft projects and bills to be worked on.

It is always good to plan every day but you also find that it's a good feeling to make advance planning on short and long term goals. This is the time to start thinking and drafting any new idea or plans that pop up in your mind. Think of new ideas, plan on implementation strategies, advantage and disadvantages expected. Pursue them as the mission continues. Always be positive in your planning for it stirs the energy to move on with the implementation.

Set your goals straight

How do you plan / make your plans?

....

Are they all piled up in your memory? Or do you write them down?

....

You need to write them down to empty your memory and to create room for new ideas. This process helps with stress relief process too.

Main emphasis up to this moment is The power in Saving.

We are in financial journey discovery series of actual self. You are the person in question. Days are passing by, things are happening in different ways. We all have different wishes and needs to take care of. Take a moment now and evaluate exactly what you want to accomplish in the next week, in 3 months, in 1 year.

You have to have a purpose in life. It can be a dream. Write it down, work on it. Remember you are the author of your life. That's the beginning of success as you also pray about it. This works better if you are traveling through that path with someone to put you on check. Who will be the person? More blessings received when you help lift each other up.

It's upon you NOW to take control and make THAT CHANGE you need. Comfort starts with proper budgeting and planning. It's through budgeting that we get a little treat when we have some change to spend in things like comfortable life, vacation and all the good things we long for. You MUST have a reason for SAVING. Some of the factors to consider can be short or long term options for saving that include; Emergency purposes, Down payment for a house, child's education, starting a business, Retirement plans, vacations and many others.

Short -term options that can easily be converted into cash include; Savings account, Shares in money market, mutual funds, treasury bills and commercial papers.

Long-term options include; Bonds, Common stocks, Plant / Equipment Estate, among others.

Note that in Long-term options in some cases, it's not a guarantee that at the end of the investment period, you will GAIN on your returns. Chances of losing are also high. So watch out lest you are caught unawares if all your money invested is gone. Investment is all about risk taking. Do not put all your eggs in one basket. Spread your risks.

Bonds / Stocks with high return in most cases are high-risk investments and vice-versa. You can form a portfolio with a combination of Low and high-risk bonds / Stocks. Always ask for the performance of the returns in the portfolio you have, and if need, be adjust if you are being faced with more risk. This will minimize your losses before you end up losing everything.

Now take a moment and think of what you would like to achieve in life.

Do you have a purpose in life?

....
....
...

Give yourself a period to work with on goals expected.

List your Short-term goals and duration for implementation;

....
....
....
....
....
....

List your Long-term goals and duration for implementation.

....
....
....
....
....
....

Day 6

Savings Mission
Resolutions

Day 6
Savings mission resolutions

At this point, it is DECISION TIME, time to make a change in your financial life.

Do you know that all our toiling and hustling is money related to helping us find a way to support ourselves and live comfortably?

Let's change our perception in Money talk. Talk to your subconscious mind to allow YOU to open up and manage your FINANCES. I know one might be wondering why ALL emphasis is on savings! Having a little CHANGE in life gives one freedom in so many ways. In this instance, it will enable you to start thinking beyond your little financial challenges. You will feel that you have a cushion to bounce back on. You will be able to start talking about investment and consider any opportunity that comes your way. You will also be able to budget and plan ahead based on what you can accomplish after viewing your savings schedule and balance at hand.

FINANCIAL "STIGMA"!

Talking about Finances doesn't really mean you got it ALL together.

Talking about Finances means you are ready to let go the stigma and take control of your Financial life by participating in planning. Best planning formula is to have all financial related issues written down, calculated, separating monthly constant expenses against income and anticipated expenses.

Hint: Stop making all calculations in your memory....you are overloading it, blocking or leaving less space for new ideas. Get a pen and a paper / book and Start writing.

Remember that you should not wait to pay all your debts before you start saving. Savings should be like your monthly rent that must be paid that comes in handy as emergency funds.

Growth

Growth involves dreaming. Dream and dream Loud. That shows a working mind. Most PROGRESS comes From WHAT was Initially A dream. As you focus on savings start planning and researching on what you want to FIRST invest in. It can be land, shares, insurance, retirement plan, building, buying a car, buying a house, school fees, vacation, e.t.c

Make a budget

This moment, write down your daily /weekly /monthly spending habit including constant bills.

....
....
....
....
....
....
....

What's your target?

This is where you need to list what you would like to achieve, when you would like to achieve it, and how you will plan on the process of working towards achieving it.

— (list at least 3)?

What?..
..

When?..
..

How?..
..

What?..
..

When?..
..

How?..
..

What?..
..

When?..
..

How?..
..

Change

Change is a process, CAN BE INSTANT OR GRADUAL. What "bad habit" would you like to stop this week in your financial journey? Just pick one or two, write it down on a piece of paper and stick it next to an area you can easily read. It can be next to your bed, on the fridge, sticky note board, next to your computer. This will act as a daily reminder to keep you on toes. Let's practice this reminder every week and review the results end of   each   week.

Day 7

Make a Step of
Faith

Day 7
Make a Step of Faith

It's been a wonderful six days of self-realization. It is at this point that you need to make your first savings deposit even if it's in the lowest amount possible. Remember a building starts with one laid down stone and its completion is a gradual process to have a visual building. It can be a penny, a nickel, a dollar, make it happen. It's a time of complete change in your life.

Do you have any accounts at this point? If you do not have any account then make a move today and make an inquiry on what you need to do to open one. There are many options available to be considered. For students consider free options offered for students. Make inquiry at the bank. Other types of accounts are current accounts, savings account, fixed deposit accounts, online current and savings account, among others.

If you have a problem with saving, consider locked savings options like fixed deposit accounts, buying shares, joining Sacco, online savings, automatic transfer to a remote bank, and any other option that might work for you.

What do Savings mean in this context?

It means that you should at least have some emergency funds literally set aside, saved for emergency use or future investment plans. NOTE...IF you have stopped spending and not literally taking the money to save it aside then you are still not getting it. You need to have a savings account for this mission with that money in it.

If you do not have any account, you can start with a piggy bank in the house. Make sure you get a tightly enclosed container that you will not be tempted to open anytime when you feel like spending without planning. I started with a piggy bank that was tightly closed, no opening on the back side too. This disciplined me to save no matter what. I had no count of what was going on in there. I made it a habit to at least throw in a penny or a dollar whenever I had some change.

I remember very well when I started saving when I moved to this country, I didn't have a job. I was a student at that time. So during sport seasons, different universities could come into our school to play or practice. What I loved most that I discovered was the fact that after games, I realized people threw a lot of pennies on the ground. I didn't know if that was some games traditions or not. That was my celebration moments. I could wait till the crowd reduces then pick up the pennies from the ground. I could gather a lot of pennies. I used that as my source of income for a certain period of time.

My kids and I still pick pennies up to this moment. They add up. Lots of pennies tend to float around so don't ignore pennies, they build up the foundation to success.

Savings Tips

Set a limit/target and choose what can motivate you. If you reach your target, push it a little higher. Work up your mind and explore more ways to get to the higher target, and KEEP Going. Works like better job searching.

Savings Strategies

Below, you will find a sample of a format to help start the process. Pick a target. How much will you want to save by the end of the year?
Keep $2 per week =$104
Keep $10 per week =$520
Keep $20 per week =$1040
Keep $100 per week=$5200

(You can adjust the figures to fit your selection which can be per day, per week, per month or whenever money is received).

In KSHS.
Savings strategy for the year can be;
Keep
Kshs.100 per week=Kshs. 5200
Kshs. 200 per week=kshs.10,400
Kshs. 500 per week=kshs. 26,000
Kshs.1000 per week=Kshs. 52,000
Kshs. 2000 per week=Kshs. 104,000
(You can adjust it accordingly but try to save a little something if your set target is not working out).

Which saving option did you settle on?

....

What is your initial deposit?

....

These are baby steps to learn to save and cut down expenses to help get some change to put aside for savings.

You also need to look for more ways to boost your income by doing some side hustle business. Bear in mind to keep working on a daily budget to help monitor your spending habits. Think outside the box; settle on a figure and start working on it after making the VERY FIRST INITIAL DEPOSIT TODAY.

FINANCIAL HIKERS KIDS VERSION!

Let US not forget about having our kids in Financial journey, let's learn together. Your kid can be your partner in the journey. Talk, plan, budget and save with them with a purpose in mind...that way they get to grow with the mindset to focus and spend wisely.

The Power Of Spoken Words Of Affirmation!

In all you do, be positive, think positive and speak positively, for they all lead to the final impact of your productivity.

References

http://www.merriam-webster.com/dictionary/self%E2%80%93analysis

About the Author

Sharon Adundo is a mother, a mentor, an Entrepreneur, Financial Educator and Founder of Financial Hikers group. She is a graduate of Dallas Baptist University (U.S.A) with a Master's degree in Finance. She also holds a first degree in Fine Arts (Kenya), with a major in Graphics Design. She possesses magnitude experience in business with over ten years' experience in the trucking industry. Currently, she is the CEO of Experalda Chain Logistics LLC, a trucking company based in Arlington, TX and also the Director of Besh Collections a boutique collection in Arlington, TX.

In 2015, Sharon Launched the Financial Hikers group on Facebook with the Focus of Empowering women globally in their financial life challenges. As a result, there was a quest for more financial information and resources. In response, in 2016, Sharon launched this NEW CHALLENGE BOOK titled "WHERE IS MY MONEY GOING?" This was a new goal to reach every age group to enable them make self-evaluation and preparation of taking full responsibility of their financial life in seven days as a startup Journey.

While not working, Sharon volunteers in charity activities within the community and back in Kenya and also participating in the fundraising drives.

Sharon also loves traveling and always traveled on a budget to trips within the USA and Africa.

www.ingramcontent.com/pod-product-compliance
Lightning Source LLC
Chambersburg PA
CBHW070921210326
41521CB00010B/2269